core belief™

Bible Study Series
for junior high/middle school

THE TRUTH ABOUT
Sharing Faith

Group
Loveland, Colorado

The Truth About Sharing Faith

Core Belief Bible Study Series

Copyright © 1998 Group Publishing, Inc.

Credits

Editor: Karl Leuthauser
Creative Development Editors: Ivy Beckwith and Paul Woods
Chief Creative Officer: Joani Schultz
Copy Editor: Shirley Michaels
Art Director: Ray Tollison
Cover Art Director: Jeff A. Storm
Computer Graphic Artist/Illustrator: Eris Klein
Photographer: Jafe Parsons and Craig DeMartino
Production Manager: Gingar Kunkel

ISBN 0-7644-0873-9

10 9 8 7 6 5 4 3 2 1   07 06 05 04 03 02 01 00 99 98

Printed in the United States of America.

Bible Study Series
for junior high/middle school

contents:

the Core Belief: ▼ Sharing Faith

As our relationship with God grows, we will naturally want to share what we have with others. We can use all we have at our disposal to communicate God's great love and sacrifice to those who don't know him. We can use our lives by loving others and living righteously. We can communicate God's love through our words by telling our faith stories and telling others about Jesus Christ.

We can't force others to make a commitment to Jesus Christ. Only the Holy Spirit can do the work in people's hearts to give them the desire to give their lives to Christ. But we can do our part. Through the studies in this Core Christian Belief, young people can realize their natural desire to share Christ with those around them. And they can discover how to do this in respectful, loving ways.

the ▼ Helpful Stuff

the ▼Studies

▼Sharing Faith
as a Core Christian Belief

Sharing your faith in Christ doesn't just mean telling someone how to become a Christian. It can also mean asking God to give you the strength to live a life that would draw someone to him. It means caring for people's needs and leaning on God to give you the right words at the right time. And it means letting the Holy Spirit strengthen you when you've done all you can.

Teenagers can share their faith wherever they go. The first study of this book will help kids see that **school** can be their first mission field. While at school, they can share faith actively as well as through the way they live.

The second study will help kids put their **faith in action**. It will challenge them to go beyond their comfort zones and to go for the extreme in their passion for sharing Christ with others. They'll be reminded that God's Spirit can work through them to make a difference.

The third study of this book will give kids some of the basic tools necessary to share their faith. They will be encouraged to use a variety of methods for **sharing faith** and will be reminded that God helps them talk about their faith.

The final study will help students deal with and understand the **persecution** they are bound to encounter when they reach out to others with the gospel. They will find that sharing their faith isn't always easy and that doing so sometimes requires a price.

Kids need to know that sharing their faith with others isn't just a religious duty. When God opens kids' hearts to help them see all that he's done for them, sharing their faith with others will be a natural outward expression of their lives as Christians. And their lives will change as they demonstrate their faith through their words and their actions.

*For a more comprehensive look at this Core Christian Belief, read Group's **Get Real: Making Core Christian Beliefs Relevant to Teenagers.***

DEPTH FINDER

HOW THE BIBLE DESCRIBES SHARING FAITH

To help you effectively guide your kids toward this Core Christian Belief, use these overviews as a launching point for a more in-depth study of sharing faith.

● **We should be motivated to share our faith with others because of what God has done for us.** Sharing our faith isn't a matter of obligation, but a natural outgrowth of a maturing relationship with God. As we understand what God has done for us and as we realize the fate of those who don't have a personal relationship with him, our natural response is an outpouring of love toward others. Since we have found the greatest treasure in the world, we want those around us to have it, too (Matthew 13:44-45; Luke 15:8-10; Romans 9:1-5; 1 Thessalonians 2:8; and 1 John 4:19).

● **We share our faith through the way we live.** When we become Christians, we automatically become representatives of Christ here on earth. Non-Christians form images of what Christians are and of who our God is based on what they see us do. Therefore, as we seek to obey God, we demonstrate our faith through our lives in these ways:

By demonstrating God's love—God is the source of all love and wants his love to flow through us to others. As we show love for others, we demonstrate that we're truly Jesus' followers (Matthew 25:34-40; Luke 6:31-35; John 13:34-35; Romans 13:9-10; 1 Thessalonians 3:12; and 1 John 4:7-8, 16).

By living a pure life—Jesus lived a pure, honest, sinless life. We're to follow his example by living pure lives so that no one can question our honesty or integrity. If we keep our lives free from dishonest or immoral actions, people can't legitimately form negative opinions about Christianity because of us. In fact, our honesty and integrity may encourage others to ask why we live the way we do (1 Kings 9:4; 2 Corinthians 8:20-21; Titus 2:2-15; Hebrews 4:15; and 1 Peter 2:11-12; 3:13-16).

● **We share our faith through our words.** Our actions may draw people toward Christ, but only through our words will they be able to understand and accept the gift God offers through Jesus. We need to be able to articulate what Jesus means to us, and we need to be ready to tell others how they, too, can receive God's gift of eternal life. We can verbally share our faith in several ways:

By telling our faith stories—When people become interested in why we're different from the crowd, we need to tell them what Jesus means in our lives. When they hear what Jesus has done for us, they'll be better able to believe in what Jesus can do for them (Luke 8:38-39; John 4:28-29, 39-42, 9:20-27; 1 Timothy 1:12-17; and 1 Peter 3:15).

By telling others about Jesus—This is the heart of sharing our faith. We're to be ready to tell others what Jesus has done in dying as the sacrifice for our sins and how we can have eternal life through him. We cannot, however, convince people to accept God's gift of eternal life. That's the role of the Holy Spirit in their lives (Matthew 28:19-20; John 16:7-11; Acts 1:8; 3:1-26; 4:8-12; 8:1b-4; 16:29-34; 1 Corinthians 2:9-10; 15:1-4; and 1 Thessalonians 1:4-6).

CORE CHRISTIAN BELIEF OVERVIEW

Here are the twenty-four Core Christian Belief categories that form the backbone of Core Belief Bible Study Series:

The Nature of God	Jesus Christ	The Holy Spirit
Humanity	Evil	Suffering
Creation	The Spiritual Realm	The Bible
Salvation	Spiritual Growth	Personal Character
God's Justice	Sin & Forgiveness	The Last Days
Love	The Church	Worship
Authority	Prayer	Family
Service	Relationships	Sharing Faith

Look for Group's Core Belief Bible Study Series books in these other Core Christian Beliefs!

about core belief

Bible Study Series
for junior high/middle school

Think for a moment about your young people. When your students walk out of your youth program after they graduate from junior high or high school, what do you want them to know? What foundation do you want them to have so they can make wise choices?

You probably want them to know the essentials of the Christian faith. You want them to base everything they do on the foundational truths of Christianity. Are you meeting this goal?

If you have any doubt that your kids will walk into adulthood knowing and living by the tenets of the Christian faith, then you've picked up the right book. All the books in Group's Core Belief Bible Study Series encourage young people to discover the essentials of Christianity and to put those essentials into practice. Let us explain...

What Is Group's Core Belief Bible Study Series?

Group's Core Belief Bible Study Series is a biblically in-depth study series for junior high and senior high teenagers. This Bible study series utilizes four defining commitments to create each study. These "plumb lines" provide structure and continuity for every activity, study, project, and discussion. They are:

● **A Commitment to Biblical Depth**—Core Belief Bible Study Series is founded on the belief that kids not only *can* understand the deeper truths of the Bible but also *want* to understand them. Therefore, the activities and studies in this series strive to explain the "why" behind every truth we explore. That way, kids learn principles, not just rules.

● **A Commitment to Relevance**—Most kids aren't interested in abstract theories or doctrines about the universe. They want to know how to live successfully right now, today, in the heat of problems they can't ignore. Because of this, each study connects a real-life need with biblical principles that speak directly to that need. This study series finally bridges the gap between Bible truths and the real-world issues kids face.

● **A Commitment to Variety**—Today's young people have been raised in a sound bite world. They demand variety. For that reason, no two meetings in this study series are shaped exactly the same.

● **A Commitment to Active and Interactive Learning**—Active learning is learning by doing. Interactive learning simply takes active learning a step further by having kids teach each other what they've learned. It's a process that helps kids internalize and remember their discoveries.

For a more detailed description of these concepts, see the section titled "Why Active and Interactive Learning Works With Teenagers" beginning on page 57.

So how can you accomplish all this in a set of four easy-to-lead Bible studies? By weaving together various "power" elements to produce a fun experience that leaves kids challenged and encouraged.

THE ISSUE: Relationships

Betrayed!

HELPING KIDS DEAL WITH REJECTION FROM THE PEOPLE THEY LOVE

by Jennifer Cornell

THE POINT:

God is love.

■ Betrayal has very little shock value for this generation. It's as commonplace as compact discs and mosh pits. For many kids today, betrayal characterizes their parents' wedding vows. It's part of their curriculum at school; it defines the headlines and evening news. Betrayal is not only accepted—it's expected. ■ At the heart of such acceptance lies the belief that nothing is absolute. No vow, no law, no promise can be trusted. Relationships are betrayed at the earliest convenience. Repeatedly, kids see that something called "love" lasts just as long as it's [...] permanence. But deep inside, they hunger to see a [...]

The Study AT A GLANCE

SECTION	MINUTES	WHAT STUDENTS WILL DO	SUPPLIES
Discussion Starter	up to 5	JUMP-START—Identify some of the most common themes in today's movies.	Newsprint, marker
Investigation of Betrayal	12 to 15	REALITY CHECK—Form groups to compare anonymous, real-life stories of betrayal with experiences in their own lives.	"Profiles of Betrayal" handouts (p. 20), highlighter pens, newsprint, marker, tape
	3 to 5	WHO BETRAYED WHOM?—Guess the identities of the people profiled in the handouts.	Paper, tape, pen
Investigation of True Love	15 to 18	SOURCE WORK—Study and discuss God's definition of perfect love.	Bibles, newsprint, marker
	5 to 7	LOVE MESSAGES—Create unique ways to send a "message of love" to the victims of betrayal they've been studying.	Newsprint, markers, tape
Personal Application	10 to 15	SYMBOLIC LOVE—Give a partner a personal symbol of perfect love.	Paper lunch sack, pens, scissors, paper, catalogs

notes:

● **A Relevant Topic**—More than ever before, kids live in the now. What matters to them and what attracts their hearts is what's happening in their world at this moment. For this reason, every Core Belief Bible Study focuses on a particular hot topic that kids care about.

● **A Core Christian Belief**—Group's Core Belief Bible Study Series organizes the wealth of Christian truth and experience into twenty-four Core Christian Belief categories. These twenty-four headings act as umbrellas for a collection of detailed beliefs that define Christianity and set it apart from the world and every other religion. Each book in this series features one Core Christian Belief with lessons suited for junior high or senior high students.

"But," you ask, "won't my kids be bored talking about all these spiritual beliefs?" No way! As a youth leader, you know the value of using hot topics to connect with young people. Ultimately teenagers talk about issues because they're searching for meaning in their lives. They want to find the one equation that will make sense of all the confusing events happening around them. Each Core Belief Bible Study answers that need by connecting a hot topic with a powerful Christian principle. Kids walk away from the study with something more solid than just the shifting ebb and flow of their own opinions. They walk away with a deeper understanding of their Christian faith.

● **The Point**—This simple statement is designed to be the intersection between the Core Christian Belief and the hot topic. Everything in the study ultimately focuses on The Point so that kids study it and allow it time to sink into their hearts.

● **The Study at a Glance**—A quick look at this chart will tell you what kids will do, how long it will take them to do it, and what supplies you'll need to get it done.

● The Bible Connection—This is the power base of each study. Whether it's just one verse or several chapters, The Bible Connection provides the vital link between kids' minds and their hearts. The content of each Core Belief Bible Study reflects the belief that the true power of God—the power to expose, heal, and change kids' lives—is contained in his Word.

THE POINT OF *BETRAYED!*:

God is love.

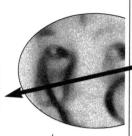

THE BIBLE CONNECTION

1 JOHN 4:7-21   The Apostle John explains the nature and definition of perfect love.

In this study, kids will compare the imperfect love defined in real-life stories of betrayal to God's definition of perfect love.

By making this comparison, kids can discover that God is love and therefore incapable of betraying them. Then they'll be able to recognize the incredible opportunity God off... relationship worthy of their absolute trust.

Explore the verses in The Bible Connection... mation in the Depthfinder boxes throughout... understanding of how these Scriptures conne...

LEADER TIP

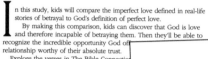

DISCUSSION STARTER ▼

Jump-Start (up to 5 minutes) As kids arrive, ask them to think... common themes in movies, books, TV show... have kids each contribute ideas for a mas... two other kids in the room and sharing their fi... sider providing copies of People magazine to l... what's currently showing on television or at the... their suggestions, write their respon... on new... **come up with a lot of great idea... Even tho... ent, look through this list and... ry to discov... ments most of these themes... have in comm...**

After kids make several su... estions, mention... responses are connected wi... the idea of betra...

● Why do you think... etrayal is such a co...

Betrayed! 17

LEADER TIP for The Study Because this topic can be so powerful and relevant to kids' lives, your group members may be tempted to get caught up in issues and lose sight of the deeper biblical principle found in The Point. Help your kids grasp The Point by guiding kids to focus on the biblical investigation and discussing how God's truth connects with reality in their lives.

DEPTHFINDER UNDERSTANDING INTEGRITY

Your students may not be entirely familiar with the meaning of integrity, especially as it might apply to God's character in the Trinity. Use these definitions (taken from Webster's II New Riverside Dictionary) and other information to help you guide kids toward a better understanding of how God maintains integrity through the three expressions of the Trinity.

Integrity: 1. Firm adherence to a code or standard of values. 2. The state of being unimpaired. 3. The quality or condition of being undivided.

Synonyms for integrity include probity, completeness, wholeness, soundness, and perfection.

Our word "integrity" comes from the Latin word *integritas*, which means soundness. *Integritas* is also the root of the word "integer," which means "whole or complete," as in a "whole" number.

The Hebrew word that's often translated "integrity" (for example, in Psalm 25:21 [NIV]) is *tam*. It means whole, perfect, sincere, and honest.

CREATIVE GOD-EXPLORATION ▼

Top Hats (18 to 20 minutes) Form three groups, with each trio member from the previous activity going to a different group. Give each group Bibles, paper, and pens, and assign each group a different hat God wears: Father, Son, or Holy Spirit. ... their goal is to write one list describing what God does in the... ... God's character...

● Depthfinder Boxes—These informative sidelights located throughout each study add insight into a particular passage, word, historical fact, or Christian doctrine. Depthfinder boxes also provide insight into teen culture, adolescent development, current events, and philosophy.

● Leader Tips—These handy information boxes coach you through the study, offering helpful suggestions on everything from altering activities for different-sized groups to streamlining discussions to using effective discipline techniques.

Holy Profiles

Your assigned Bible passage describes how a particular person or group responded when confronted with God's holiness. Use the information in your passage to help your group discuss the questions below. Then use your flashlights to teach the other two groups what you discover.

■ Based on your passage, what does holiness look like?

■ What does holiness sound like?

■ When people see God's holiness, how does it affect them?

■ How is this response to God's holiness like humility?

■ Based on your passage, how would you describe humility?

■ Why is humility an appropriate human response to God's holiness?

■ Based on what you see in your passage, do you think you are a humble person? Why or why not?

■ What's one way you could develop humility in your life this week?

● Handouts—Most Core Belief Bible Studies include photocopiable handouts to use with your group. Handouts might take the form of a fun game, a lively discussion starter, or a challenging study page for kids to take home—anything to make your study more meaningful and effective.

The Last Word on Core Belief Bible Studies

Soon after you begin to use Group's Core Belief Bible Study Series, you'll see signs of real growth in your group members. Your kids will gain a deeper understanding of the Bible and of their own Christian faith. They'll see more clearly how a relationship with Jesus affects their daily lives. And they'll grow closer to God.

But that's not all. You'll also see kids grow closer to one another.

That's because this series is founded on the principle that Christian faith grows best in the context of relationship. Each study uses a variety of interactive pairs and small groups and always includes discussion questions that promote deeper relationships. The friendships kids will build through this study series will enable them to grow *together* toward a deeper relationship with God.

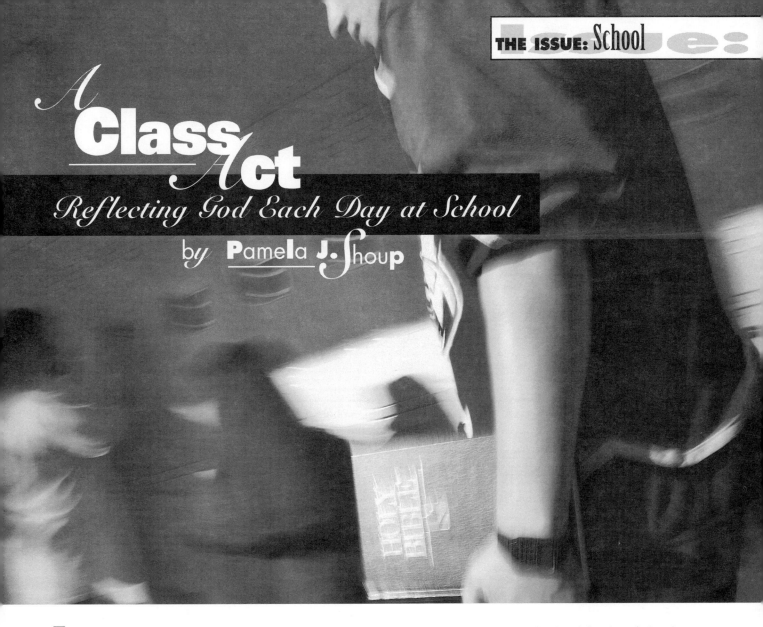

A Class Act

Reflecting God Each Day at School

by Pamela J. Shoup

■ School, especially junior high school, can be a rough place. A student feels picked on by a teacher. Cliques form, and inevitably someone feels excluded. No matter how hard some students study, they can't raise their grades. And don't forget that young people face drugs, sexual temptations, gangs, and guns at school. ■ How do your students handle these situations? When others know that a young person is a Christian, they watch that young person to learn more about God. Classmates, custodians, teachers, and principals wait to see how Christian students respond to tough and unfair situations. Will your students' responses draw others near to God or push them away? ■ This study invites your young people to evaluate whether they represent God well at school. Through this evaluation, your students can discover how to share God with class.

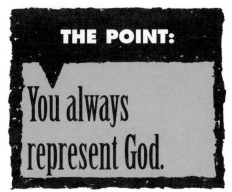

THE POINT:

You always represent God.

The Study
AT A GLANCE

SECTION	MINUTES	WHAT STUDENTS WILL DO	SUPPLIES
Tower Creation	up to 10	TOWER OF TERROR—Build a tower representing what they dislike about school.	Bibles, boxes of assorted sizes, black markers
School Simulation	40 to 45	COOL SCHOOL—Attend "classes" about real-life school situations and complete projects representing their responses to those situations.	Bibles, "Cool School" handouts (pp. 22-24), paper, pencils, vinegar, baking soda, jar, teaspoon, bucket or large bowl, tape
Reflection	up to 10	IN GOD'S IMAGE—Share how they represented God during the previous activity.	Bibles, newsprint, marker, tape

notes:

THE POINT OF "A CLASS ACT":

You always represent God.

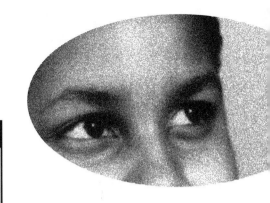

THE BIBLE CONNECTION

MATTHEW 7:7-8	Jesus explains that those who seek him will find him.
MATTHEW 11:28-30	Jesus promises rest to all who come to him with heavy loads.
MARK 8:35-38	Jesus explains that we must put him first.
LUKE 21:10-19	Jesus tells his disciples that they will face persecution.
ROMANS 12:4-10	This passage encourages us to honor others.
1 CORINTHIANS 10:31–11:1 and 2 CORINTHIANS 3:18	These passages explain how we can glorify God in everything we do.
1 CORINTHIANS 15:33-34	This verse explains that bad company corrupts good character.

I n this study, kids will share what they dislike about school. Then they'll attend "classes" challenging them to represent God in a variety of situations they might face at school.

By doing this, kids will discover how Christians reflect God's nature in all they do, affecting how others view and relate to God.

Explore the verses in The Bible Connection; then examine the information in the Depthfinder boxes throughout the study to gain a deeper understanding of how these Scriptures connect with your young people.

BEFORE THE STUDY

Set out two black markers and eight to ten empty boxes of various sizes. Practice stacking the boxes into a tower to make sure they won't topple during the activity.

Photocopy the "Cool School" handout (pp. 22-24). Then tape each section of the handout to a different wall of your meeting room. Leave a Bible at each station. At Station 1, set up a table, and place on it a bottle of vinegar, a box of baking soda, a teaspoon, an empty glass jar, and a bucket or large bowl.

LEADER TIP
for The Study

Because this topic can be so powerful and relevant to kids' lives, your group members may be tempted to get caught up in issues and lose sight of the deeper biblical principle found in The Point. Help your kids grasp The Point by guiding kids to focus on the biblical investigation and discussing how God's truth connects with reality in their lives.

LEADER TIP

for Tower of Terror

If you have eight or fewer students in your group, invite them all to participate in writing on the boxes and building the tower.

LEADER TIP

for Tower of Terror

If you have non-Christian kids at your meeting, this is a good opportunity to involve them in the discussion. Invite them to ask questions throughout the study and to meet with you after the meeting if they'd like to know more about your group, Christianity, or the Bible.

LEADER TIP

for The Study

Because this study addresses how kids represent God at school, you might want to do this study during the school year. However, it can also make a great end-of-the-summer meeting, preparing kids to represent God when they go back to school.

THE STUDY

TOWER CREATION ▼

Tower of Terror (up to 10 minutes) As kids arrive, have them find partners and discuss things they like and dislike about school. Once everyone has arrived, say: **Today we're going to talk about school. Some of you like school and do well, and some of you probably struggle or just don't like school at all. Let's build a tower representing what you dislike most about school, based on the discussion you just had with your partner.**

Have kids form a circle on the floor around the boxes you collected before class. Recruit two volunteers to be Recorders and two more to be Builders. Ask:

● **What do you dislike most about school?**

Listen to kids' responses, and pick the one that seems to be most popular. Have a Recorder use a black marker to write that response on the side of the largest box in the pile. Continue this activity quickly, having Recorders take turns writing students' responses on smaller and smaller boxes. As Recorders write on the boxes, have Builders use the completed boxes to create a tower.

DEPTH FINDER   UNDERSTANDING THESE KIDS

Bill Sanders, author of *School Daze: Helping Parents Cope With the Bewildering World of Public Schools*, surveyed 7,500 teenagers in seventh through twelfth grades to find out the greatest problems that today's young people face. The category that got the most response was school/grades/homework. (Over 36 percent of the respondents expressed this concern.)

But students were also concerned about peer pressure. (Twenty percent of the respondents expressed this concern.) According to Sanders' survey, students felt peer pressure the most in the areas of alcohol, drugs, and sex. The survey showed that over 34 percent of teenagers felt pressured by their friends to drink alcohol and almost 23 percent felt pressured to do drugs. Close to 20 percent have been pressured to have sex. Other peer pressure areas included appearance/clothes, school/grades, smoking, fitting in/popularity, and sports.

You can encourage your young people to represent God and to share their faith in the midst of all these challenges and pressures. During your meeting times, discuss these issues, and explore Scriptures that help kids discover how they can represent God in their choices. In addition to the Scriptures offered in this study, you might hold Bible studies on the topics of studying (Proverbs 2:1-10), peer pressure (Psalm 1), popularity (Mark 9:30-37), and self-esteem (1 Corinthians 12:1-11).

Say: **Here's our Tower of Terror representing all the problems you face at school every day.** Ask:

● **How do you feel when you look at this tower?**

● **How is that feeling like how you feel about school? How is it different?**

Have kids form trios, read Matthew 11:28-30, and discuss these questions:

● **What does Jesus promise to those who carry heavy loads?**

● **How can we have what Jesus promises?**

● **How does Jesus' promise affect how you feel when you look at our Tower of Terror? how you feel about school in general?**

● **What's one specific way Jesus can help you deal with the problems you face at school?**

Say: **Today we're going to learn that no matter how bad things get at school, you always represent God. The way**  you approach school challenges reflects God's nature to those around you. Let's go to "school" to learn more about this truth.

LEADER TIP
for The Study

Whenever groups discuss a list of questions, write the list on newsprint, and tape it to the wall so groups can discuss the questions at their own pace.

SCHOOL SIMULATION ▼

Cool School (40 to 45 minutes)
Say: **You're going to go to school in this room. Each of the stations represents a different "class." But these classes are different from the usual classes you take. Your "cool school" classes will be in peer pressure, cheating, cliques, and racial tension.**

Have students form four groups, and give each group pencils and four sheets of paper. Send each group to one of the four stations you prepared before the study. Say: **Follow the directions posted at your station. Read the situation, discuss the questions, and complete the "class project." You have eight minutes.**

After eight minutes, call: **Switch classes**, and have students rotate clockwise to the next class.

After groups have visited all four classes, call them back together, and say: **OK, this is the last class of the day. It's wisdom class. First, let's share the projects you did in each class.** Invite groups to share the projects that describe their responses to the situation presented in the peer pressure class. Then do the same for the other three classes.

Read aloud 1 Corinthians 10:31–11:1; then ask:

● **What does this passage say about how you always represent God?**

● **How well have you followed Christ's example in your responses to the situations on peer pressure, cheating, cliques, and racial tension?**

● **How can you glorify God in all you do?**

Have everyone read aloud and in unison Matthew 7:7-8.

Say: **God will help you represent him well—all you have to do is ask him to help you. When you face temptations, ask Jesus to help you resist them. When you're scared or anxious, ask God**

LEADER TIP
for Cool School

If you have fewer than twelve kids, have students form two or three groups. If you have more than twenty-eight students, have students form groups of four or less, and have more than one group go to each station at a time. Increase the supplies for the peer pressure class as necessary. If possible, assign one adult to each station. If you're short of help, assign an adult at the peer pressure class to supervise the science experiment.

for courage and peace. When someone treats you badly, ask God to help you love that person. Remember, <u>you always represent God</u>.

Let's stand in a circle, hold hands, and pray together. When students are ready, pray: **Dear God, we ask for your guidance and help as we face problems at school. Please give us the wisdom to make the right decisions, and help us always to represent you well at school and in the rest of our lives. Amen.**

REFLECTION ▼

LEADER TIP
for In God's Image

If you have a class of twenty or more kids, have kids form two or three groups and do this activity in their groups.

In God's Image (up to 10 minutes)
Say: **Today you've discovered that <u>you always represent God</u>. If you have faith in Jesus, God will help you represent him well, even when things at school get difficult.**

Let's explore how you can live your life every day in God's image.

Have a volunteer lie down on a large sheet of newsprint; then trace his or her outline on the newsprint with a marker. Tape the newsprint to a wall.

Have another volunteer read aloud 2 Corinthians 3:18. Say: **Let's review the classes you went to today and determine when you chose to show the Lord's glory and become like him. As you name ways you represented God, let's write them on the outline. For example, if you decided to say a kind word about a friend that other kids were putting down, one of you would write "say a kind word" on the mouth of the outline.**

Before dismissing kids, have them return to their partners from the opening activity. Have students express one way their partners represent God in everyday life.

"So whether you eat or drink

do it all for

DEPTHFINDER — RELIGION IN PUBLIC SCHOOLS

Why is there a public outcry when a chaplain prays at a graduation ceremony or a student wants to form an on-campus Bible study? Why do Christian students end up in Supreme Court attempting to defend their rights?

According to Judith Winston of the U.S. Department of Education (quoted in Christianity Today magazine), school administrators are often cautious when dealing with religious issues on campus, limiting expression instead of allowing it. Colleen Pinyan, public affairs coordinator for the Rutherford Institute (a religious liberty advocacy group), disagrees. Quoted in the Baptist Press, Pinyan claims that "the main problem is that courts have not consistently produced decisions that fully protect religious freedom." How does this debate affect your kids as they seek to represent God at school? They have a right to religious expression in the United States, but they may find themselves challenged by teachers and school administrators. Educate your students on their rights, and support them as they exercise those rights. Also encourage students to be proactive. For example, if your students want to host a Bible study on their school grounds, encourage them to find out school rules regarding Bible studies, such as where and when they can meet. Challenge your students to positively represent God to school officials by the loving and respectful way they assert their rights.

(Sources compiled from Christianity Online © 1995.)

"...or whatever you do, the glory of God." —1 CORINTHIANS 10:31

COOL School

Photocopy this handout, and tape each of the four sections to a different wall of your meeting room.

PEER PRESSURE

Read the following situation; then discuss the questions, and follow the instructions below.

You run around with kids who drink alcohol, smoke cigarettes, and occasionally smoke pot. You don't like doing any of these things, and your parents would go crazy if they knew what your friends do. But these people are your friends, and you don't want to lose them. You join them in an occasional cigarette and drink because if you don't, your friends might think you're not cool.

DISCUSS THESE QUESTIONS:

• What would you do in this situation?

• Read 1 Corinthians 15:33-34. What does this Scripture say about the friends you choose? about how you should respond to peer pressure?

• What are a few ways that peer pressure can be positive?

CONDUCT THIS SIMPLE SCIENCE EXPERIMENT WITH THE SUPPLIES PROVIDED.

Pour a little vinegar in a jar, and add a teaspoon of baking soda. Pour out the mixture when finished, and discuss these questions:

• How is the reaction of the vinegar and baking soda like positive or negative peer pressure?

• How can you always represent God when facing peer pressure?

Decide as a group how you'd respond to the situation described above, write it on a piece of paper, and label it "Peer Pressure." Take the paper with you as you go to the next class.

CHEATING

Read the following situation; then discuss the questions, and follow the instructions below.

A big science test is coming up this week, and science is your toughest class. Your best friend tells you that he has the answers to the test—he bought them from an upperclassman. Lots of kids are buying the test and will probably ace it now. If you don't get the answers, you'll really look bad with so many other kids doing well. Plus, your dad says if you don't keep your grades up, you'll have to quit the basketball team. You're considering buying the test.

DISCUSS THESE QUESTIONS:

• What would you do in this situation?

• Read Mark 8:35-38. How can cheating cause you to lose your soul?

• How can faith help you to succeed?

• How can you always represent God when taking tests and doing homework?

Decide as a group what you would do in this situation, write it on a piece of paper, and title it "Cheating." Create a simple math formula, such as "tests + cheating = ?" and write it on the paper.

CLIQUES

Read the following situation; then discuss the questions, and follow the instructions below.

You're on the fringe of the most popular clique in school. These people are really "in" and have great parties, great clothes, and plenty of boyfriends or girlfriends. Sometimes they let you hang out with them. But they say really mean things about other people. In particular, they always make fun of one of your friends who's Asian and a really good student. They seem to be drawing you in and have even invited you to a party this weekend. Still, you're not sure you want to be a part of a group that can be so mean to others.

DISCUSS THESE QUESTIONS:

• What would you do in this situation?

• Read Romans 12:9-10. According to this Scripture, how should we treat other people?

• How can you always represent God when you're with your friends?

Decide as a group what you would do in this situation, and prepare a short oral report about your response. Use at least one visual aid.

RACiAL TENSiON

Read the following situation; then discuss the questions, and follow the instructions below.

Your school is about evenly divided when it comes to white and black students. There's a lot of racial tension, and sometimes there's violence. Kids sometimes have guns or knives in their backpacks or lockers. You're black, and you have a good friend who's white, but sometimes you two are afraid to spend time together. People from both races say nasty things when they see you together, and you've both been threatened. You're considering pretending you're not friends anymore so neither of you gets hurt.

DiSCUSS THESE QUESTiONS:

• What would you do in this situation?

• Read Luke 21:10-19. How can God help you stand before enemies or people who do you wrong?

• How can you always represent God when confronted with prejudice?

Stand in a circle and hold hands. Individually, tell why the person on your left is a special and unique person.

Decide as a group what you would do in the situation described above, write it on a piece of paper, and title it "Racial Tension."

REAL-LIFE EXTREMISTS
Kids Who Live Radically for God

by Siv M. Ricketts

■ Skiing off cliffs, biking down mountains faster than most people drive, running in Death Valley in July, kayaking off a precipice into five feet of water... While some may call these things crazy, others call them extreme sports—pushing athletics to the outer limits. And even for teenagers who don't participate, these sports are wildly fun to watch. ■ But for Christians, can sharing Jesus with your friends compare? Sure! Allowing all-mighty God to work through you is incredibly extreme, sometimes just as scary and just as adventurous. The world, and maybe particularly teen culture, is often hostile to the message of Jesus Christ. But junior highers who take risks and allow God's Spirit to work through them as they touch others' lives see the awesome, life-changing power of God! ■ This study focuses on the true excitement and adventure that can be found in sharing Jesus with the world and helps kids to realize that God's Spirit can work through them.

THE POINT:

God's Spirit can work through you.

The Study
AT A GLANCE

SECTION	MINUTES	WHAT STUDENTS WILL DO	SUPPLIES
Warm-Up	20 to 25	TWO EXTREMES—Create their own extreme sports and compare the sports to representations of the average Christian life.	Athletic equipment, art supplies, Christian magazines, tape, scissors, newsprint, colored markers
The Game	25 to 30	JESUS FREAKS—Compare quotes from extreme teenagers and athletes and discuss Acts 8:26-38.	Bibles, "Extremists in Action" handouts (pp. 32-33)
Cool Down	5 to 10	EXTREME ENCOURAGEMENT—Write a personal statement of extremism and encourage others to be extreme for God.	Paper and pens

notes:

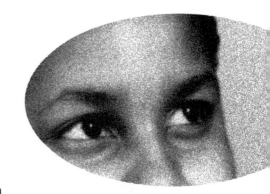

THE POINT OF "REAL-LIFE EXTREMISTS":

God's Spirit can work through you.

THE BIBLE CONNECTION

ACTS 8:26-38   Philip shares the gospel with the Ethiopian eunuch.

In this study, kids will create representations of extreme activities and examine quotes by extreme athletes and Christians to discover the similarities and differences between teen culture's and God's definitions of "extreme."

Through this experience, kids will discover that they can live extreme lifestyles by allowing God's Spirit to work through them as they share their faith in Christ with others.

Explore the verses in the Bible Connection; then study the information in the Depthfinder boxes throughout the meeting to gain a deeper understanding of how these Scriptures connect with your young people.

THE STUDY

WARM-UP ▼

Two Extremes (20 to 25 minutes) Set out sports equipment and art supplies such as balls, bats, nets, paper, pens, string, and pipe cleaners. Ask students to form groups of four; then say: **Extreme sports have become increasingly popular as people search for new dangers and thrills. What are some extreme sports you're familiar with?**

Give time for responses; then say: **Through these wildly creative sports, people stretch their minds and bodies to the limit. In your group, push the limits of your creativity to create your own extreme sport. To get started, you might think of all the aspects**

LEADER TIP for Two Extremes

You might suggest that students read the following Scripture passages as they work on what it means to be a Christian: "The Romans Road" Depthfinder (p. 29), John 3:16, and 1 John 1:8-9.

LEADER TIP

for Two Extremes

If you don't have access to Christian magazines, use a variety of types of magazines. Have kids find images from the magazines that apply to their understanding of most Christians.

LEADER TIP

for The Study

If any kids in your class are into extreme sports, arrange for them to do a demonstration as part of the meeting. Or consider planning a group outing to an extreme sporting event in advance of the study. If you have access to a VCR, you might show a video segment featuring kids involved in extreme sports. Any of these options can strengthen the impact of this meeting.

of your favorite sports and combine them to create a sport that's never been done before. You can use any of the supplies you see in the room to demonstrate or describe your sport to us.

After a few minutes, have students present their sports to the class. Ask:

● **Would you want to actually participate in the sport you created? Why or why not?**

● **Why are people attracted to the extreme?**

● **Are you attracted to danger or the extreme? Explain.**

Have students pair up with one person from their group and discuss these questions:

● **What's the most extreme thing you've ever done? ever hope to do?**

● **How do you think God feels about extreme activities?**

Have teenagers return to their groups of four, and give each group copies of recent Christian magazines such as Group, Christianity Today, Brio, Breakaway, and Vital Ministry. Give each group colored markers and a sheet of newsprint.

Say: **With your group, create a movie poster, an advertisement, a comic strip, or an illustrated story about the average Christian person. In your creation, demonstrate the strengths and weaknesses of the average Christian. Try to show what his or her life is like on a day-to-day basis.**

After about ten minutes, ask groups to share their creations. Then have groups discuss these questions:

● **Compare your creations to the extreme sports you created in the first activity. Which lifestyle seems more appealing? more exciting?**

● **Do you see the Christian life as a boring or exciting experience? Explain.**

● **What exceptions have you seen, if any?**

Say: **It might surprise you to know that we have a very extreme God. In fact, following God can lead you to a much more extreme lifestyle than you can ever imagine. <u>God's Spirit</u>**

DEPTH FINDER UNDERSTANDING THESE KIDS

It may be hard for some kids to share their faith, not because they don't want to, but because they have trouble approaching others. Steve Sjogren's *Conspiracy of Kindness* tackles this problem by allowing kids to demonstrate their faith in a way that will cause others to approach them and ask questions.

For example, kids might wash cars, mow lawns, or offer cold drinks on a hot day, all for free. People today are afraid to be vulnerable, so this type of evangelism is even more extreme because it is relational—it breaks down the walls between people by offering them deeds and not just words. Encourage your students to keep their eyes open for ways they can be extreme by sharing their faith through their actions. ("Evangelism by Deeds Which Meet Needs," Current Thoughts & Trends, January 1996.")

can work through you, and today we'll look at how his work can lead to a life of adventure. Let's pray together to ask God's Spirit to be with us as we learn more about him.

Lead students in prayer by saying: **Father, we know that your Spirit can work through us, and we ask you to direct us today as we learn more about you and how to be extreme for you. Amen.**

THE GAME ▼

Jesus Freaks

(25 to 30 minutes) Have teenagers return to their groups of four. Give each group a section of the "Extremists in Action" handout (pp. 32-33) Allow groups to read their quotes and discuss the following questions at their own pace:

- **Do you think these people are extreme? Why or why not?**
- **Are there any similarities between the quote from the Christian and the athlete? differences?**
- **What do you think about what each of them said?**
- **Which person would you most like to be? Explain.**

When groups have finished discussing their quotes, say: **While relatively few people ever take the risk of participating in extreme sports, all of you can be extreme for God. And one of the most extreme things you can do with your life is to share Jesus Christ with others. <u>God's Spirit can work through you,</u> and he wants to, but you have to let him.**

Just like the young people whose quotes you read, Philip

LEADER TIP for Jesus Freaks

If no one volunteers to share his or her personal experiences with sharing faith, ask:
- What is the most intimidating thing about sharing your faith?
- What are some simple and easy ways to share your faith with others?
- How do you start telling someone about Jesus?

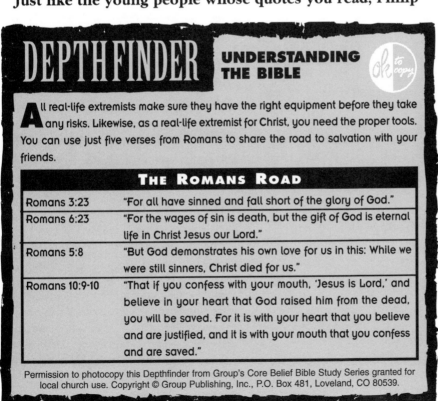

DEPTH FINDER **UNDERSTANDING THE BIBLE** *OK to copy*

All real-life extremists make sure they have the right equipment before they take any risks. Likewise, as a real-life extremist for Christ, you need the proper tools. You can use just five verses from Romans to share the road to salvation with your friends.

THE ROMANS ROAD	
Romans 3:23	"For all have sinned and fall short of the glory of God."
Romans 6:23	"For the wages of sin is death, but the gift of God is eternal life in Christ Jesus our Lord."
Romans 5:8	"But God demonstrates his own love for us in this: While we were still sinners, Christ died for us."
Romans 10:9-10	"That if you confess with your mouth, 'Jesus is Lord,' and believe in your heart that God raised him from the dead, you will be saved. For it is with your heart that you believe and are justified, and it is with your mouth that you confess and are saved."

allowed the Spirit to work through him when he met the Ethiopian eunuch. In your group, read aloud his story in Acts 8:26-38 to see how simple it can be to be extreme. Notice especially how Philip shared his faith with the eunuch.

When students have finished reading, say: **In your group, create a statement for Philip to say to the eunuch. What you would say if you had been in Philip's place? How would you explain what it means to be a Christian?**

Invite kids who have had the opportunity to share their faith with others to tell the group what happened, how they felt, and what they learned through the experience.

After students have shared their own experiences, ask:

● **Would Christianity be more exciting for you if you took more opportunities to share your faith with others? Explain.**

● **Do you think God's Spirit can work through you as he did through Philip? If so, how? If not, why not?**

● **What do you think are some other extreme things God might ask you to do for him?**

"then philip began *with that very passage of Scripture and told him the good news about Jesus."*

Acts 8:35

Extreme Encouragement (5 to 10 minutes)

Give each student a piece of paper and a pen. Say: **Even if you never win a motocross race or climb Everest, you can be a real-life extremist for God. Write your own statement about a time you were extreme for God, or describe one way that you would like to get extreme for God. Use the quotes you read earlier from Christians who allowed God's Spirit to work through them.**

Give students a minute or two to write their statements. Then have each student share his or her statement with a group of two others. Close the meeting by asking junior highers to say to the person on their left, "I know that <u>God's Spirit can work through you</u> by…" and complete the statement by describing something that person shared about his or her desire to be extreme for God.

DEPTH FINDER — UNDERSTANDING THE BIBLE

What makes a real-life extremist? A real-life extremist is someone who responds, "Here I am, Lord. Send me," no matter what God may send him or her to do. Here are some real-life extremists from Bible times:

● God called to Moses through a burning bush, and Moses responded, "Here I am." God told Moses that he was sending him to bring the Israelites out of Egypt. Even though Moses wasn't a great man or a good speaker, God went with him to free the Israelites (Exodus 3).

● Gideon didn't understand how God would use the least important member of the weakest family to save Israel. But because he was willing to obey, God used Gideon's tiny army of only three hundred men to defeat the enormous Midianite army (Judges 7).

● When Samuel was just a boy, the Lord woke him up one night to deliver a message through him to Eli, the priest. Samuel woke Eli three times before Eli understood that God was speaking to Samuel. He told Samuel to respond the next time with "Speak, Lord, for your servant is listening" (1 Samuel 3).

● Goliath laughed when he saw the young David coming to meet him in battle. Yet David cleared Israel of shame when he defeated Goliath in God's name: "I come against you in the name of the Lord Almighty, the God of the armies of Israel, whom you have defied. This day the Lord will hand you over to me" (1 Samuel 17).

● Elijah ran for his life—the people of Israel had rebelled against God, destroyed the altars, and killed the prophets. But when God asked him to go to Damascus because he had work left for him to do, Elijah went (1 Kings 19).

● Jesus prayed so earnestly the night he was arrested that he sweat blood. Three times he asked God to save him from the agony he knew awaited him. Each time, he closed his prayer with "Yet not as I will, but as you will" (Matthew 26).

These are just a few of the examples of real-life extremists in the Bible, and of these men, only Jesus was qualified to do the thing that God asked of him. The others all had perfectly logical reasons for why they weren't qualified. God doesn't necessarily choose those who have ability. He chooses those who are available.

extremists
IN ACTION

"One time, I was at a homeless shelter in New Orleans, and this guy asked me to pray for healing for his hurt back. I didn't even know if I believed in healing like that, but I prayed, and I felt something. I didn't know what to do, so finally I said, 'Amen,' and he said, 'Man, I could feel that, could you feel that? I feel great. I'm going back to work tomorrow!' And I thought, 'Okay, God, maybe You can do things. Maybe you're a little bigger than the box I put You in.'"

—Eighteen-year-old Kelly Bermudez, missionary with Youth with a Mission ("I Was a Teenage Missionary," The Grapevine, March/April 1996)

- -

"When I started, I had manicured nails and a haircut. Now I'm all grungy, I have no nails, I wear the same clothes every day. I love it! We camp out for long periods of time, and just climb. My favorite part is when you're leading, and you think, 'Oh, my rope's almost gone, I could take a big ol' whipper,' but that's the risk, the thrill."

—Moema "Mo" Clark, Eighteen-year-old rock climber (Nancy Rommelman, "Extremes," Sassy, September 1995)

"A lot of neat things are happening in my friends' lives. *Many of my friends were smoking cigarettes and weed and drinking before they started coming to cell. But God is changing their lives. I pray that all my friends will get saved...Most of my friends are Christians now and the others come to church with me on Sunday mornings."*

—Eleven-year-old Jessica Osborn, who started a Youth Cell Church in her home ("The Youngest Evangelist Speaks Out, Cell Church, Winter 1996)

"There's no future in not being scared...You've got to have *some fear of what you're doing or else you don't belong out there."*

—Twenty-nine-year-old Dean Cummings, World Extreme Skiing Champion ("Outer Limits," Newsweek, June 19, 1995)

- -

"I'm sorry it had to happen...Quitting is a bad word, and I *know that. But by quitting and breaking the commitment to the team, I feel I've fulfilled a lifelong commitment to Christ that is more important to me in the long run."*

—Seventeen-year-old Brady Phelps, supporting his controversial decision to quit the high school football team mid-season in order to concentrate on school and church (Ed Zintel, "On God's Team," The Star, November 5, 1995)

"Downhill is pretty gnarly stuff, pretty extreme. We get taken *by helicopter or chairlift to the top and bomb down. We're sprinters, going over rocks and drop-offs at 50 and 60 mph, two-wheel drifting on the edges of cliffs. Last year, I got a blow-out on a cliff going 50 and bounced over a fence. It was kamikaze."*

—Twenty-three-year-old Missy Giove, downhill mountain-bike champion (Nancy Rommelman, "Extremes," Sassy, September, 1995)

Show Me the Way

HELPING KIDS TELL OTHERS ABOUT JESUS

by Helen Turnbull and Debbie Gowensmith

■ Wendy Huisman is not just a great student and a great basketball player—she's also on a mission. She says, "Spiritually, I want people to see Jesus through me. If no one sees Christ through me, then I'm not doing what I'm supposed to be doing" (Mark Moring, "Nothing to Brag About," Campus Life, February 1996). ■ Toby Long collected ten thousand T-shirts to send to an African country where all people have to wear is what they *are* wearing. He says, "The most important thing to me is my relationship with Christ…He asked us to assist the needy…So, I'm not only able to obey him in helping my fellow human beings, but I'm also able to serve my Savior, which I like a lot" (Mark Moring, "Toby's Two Tons of T's," Campus Life, July/August 1996). ■ Lorenzo Romar is a basketball coach who cares about more than his players' dribbling and shooting skills: He cares about their lives off the court. That's why he teaches his players about God. He says, "I'm trying to teach these guys Christlike leadership skills and give them the ability to look at the world like godly men even if they don't always choose to give their lives to Christ" (Dave Geisler and Jesse Florea, "March Madness!" Breakaway, March 1996). ■ Being a Christian can be a big responsibility. We're called to share Christ with others in many ways: through our attitudes, actions, and words. Do your kids see the opportunities they have to share their faith? And do they feel confident enough to share their faith? ■ Use this study to teach your kids that evangelizing is not just for pastors; it's something every Christian does. Then help your students understand that evangelizing can be preaching on a college campus but it can also be praying for a friend in spiritual need. Use this study to give your kids the knowledge that Jesus promised he'd always be with them and that he will help them talk about their faith.

THE POINT:

God helps you talk about your faith.

The Study
AT A GLANCE

The Study at a glance

SECTION	MINUTES	WHAT STUDENTS WILL DO	SUPPLIES
Opening Operation	5 to 10	WHAT'S THAT SOUND?—Try to describe a song to each other without using certain words.	CDs, CD player with headphones, copies of the lists described in the "Before the Study" box
Evangelism Exploration	10 to 15	S.H.O.H.E.E.—Form a "support group" to discuss why sharing faith is important.	Bibles, name tags, pens, newsprint, markers, tape
	25 to 30	OPPORTUNITY KNOCKS—Move from situation to situation to discuss the best ways to share their faith.	Bibles, scissors, colored paper, newsprint, "Opportunity Knocks" handouts (p. 44), marker, tape
Closing Commitment	5 to 10	YOU, ME, AND HIM—Commit to being mentors to one another and discuss the Holy Spirit's role in faith sharing.	Bibles, paper, pens

notes:

God helps you talk about your faith.

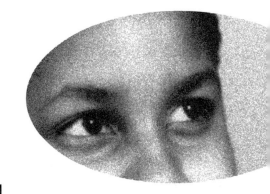

THE BIBLE CONNECTION

MATTHEW 25:31-40; EPHESIANS 5:1-2; COLOSSIANS 4:2-4; 1 PETER 3:15-16	These passages describe different ways to share faith.
MATTHEW 28:16-20	Jesus tells the disciples to tell others about him.
COLOSSIANS 4:5-6	Paul encourages followers to share their faith at every opportunity.
PHILEMON 6	Paul prays that followers will share their faith.

In this study, kids will try to describe music they listen to, form a faith-sharing "support group," experience opportunities to share their faith, and commit to being mentors to one another.

Through these experiences, kids can learn the importance of sharing their faith and specific ways to share their faith. Most important, kids can learn that God will help them talk about their faith.

Explore the verses in The Bible Connection; then examine the information in the Depthfinder boxes throughout the study to gain a deeper understanding of how these Scriptures connect with your young people.

BEFORE THE STUDY

For the "What's That Sound?" activity, bring a CD or a cassette tape of music that kids are probably not familiar with. Try to find music that has a very unique sound, such as Gregorian chant or polka music. On a sheet of paper make a list of the first six words that come to your mind when you try to describe the music. For example, if you use a Gregorian chant CD, your list might include words like monks, chant, sing, Europe, talk, and hymns. Make one copy of the list for every four teenagers in your group.

For the "Opportunity Knocks" activity, make one photocopy of the "Opportunity Knocks" handout (p. 44). Cut apart the situations on the copy, and photocopy each situation on a different color of paper. For example, you might have ten copies of situation 1 on blue paper, ten copies of situation 2 on yellow paper, and so on. Make sure you have at least one situation for every two students.

THE STUDY

OPENING OPERATION ▼

What's That Sound? (5 to 10 minutes)
As kids arrive, play Christian music they're familiar with and enjoy. Have kids form groups of four. Have each group send a volunteer to the stereo. Put a CD that kids probably aren't familiar with in the CD player. Try to find something with a unique sound such as Gregorian chant or polka.

Say to the volunteers: **I've put a different CD in the stereo. Each of you will listen to the CD for a few minutes and then describe what you heard to your group. Before you go back to your group, I'm going to give you a list of words that you *cannot* use while trying to describe what you heard. You also can't tell your group what kind of music it is or who the artist is.**

Give the volunteers the list of words you created before the study, and have them each listen to the music through headphones for

DEPTH FINDER WHY WE SHOULD SHARE OUR FAITH

Jesus told us to tell others about him. But why? What are the benefits?
● **Drawing others toward a relationship with God.** Christ came to seek and save what was lost (Luke 19:10), and we're supposed to do the same. Individuals, groups of people, and the Holy Spirit work together to accomplish this goal.

● **Helping us live as children of God.** As Christians, we are to set an example of Christ for others. When we take this responsibility seriously, our own faith will be strengthened.

● **Building a community of believers.** When several believers embrace a new Christian or a non-Christian, everyone's faith moves to a higher level. Together these people support each other, ask each other tough questions, and keep each other on the right track.

Here are some other benefits to sharing faith:
● learning to be good role models
● bringing meaning to others' lives
● deepening our personal faith
● studying the Bible
● seeing how a friend's new faith affects his or her life
● developing leadership skills
● exploring life's tough questions
● learning to love others
● listening to God
● building friendships
● taking an active role in the church

about twenty seconds. Send the volunteers back to their groups to describe what they heard without using the words on the lists you gave them.

Say: **As your volunteer tries to describe the music, I'd like you to try to figure out what kind of music it was and how it probably sounds.**

Give the volunteers one minute to describe the music. Then ask:

● **What kind of music do you think the volunteers listened to?**

● **Can you sing a few bars of the song?**

If anyone answers "yes" to the above question, ask him or her to sing. Otherwise ask:

● **Why can't you sing the song?**

Say: **I'd like you to imagine what you think the song sounds like.** Play the song so everyone can hear it; then have groups discuss these questions:

● **Did the song sound exactly as you expected?**

● **What factors affected your understanding of what the song would sound like?**

● **What factors affect people's understanding or willingness to hear the message of the gospel?**

● **How does this experience demonstrate what it's like to share your faith with those who don't believe in Jesus?**

● **What things get in the way of sharing your faith with others? with their ability to understand?**

● **What is the most difficult thing about sharing faith?**

Say: **There are all sorts of barriers you have to work through to share your faith. You have your own fears to work through. You may also have to get past the judgments others have made against Christianity. There is also a possibility that Christianity is so foreign to a person's way of thinking that he or she won't understand the terms you use. Fortunately, <u>God helps you talk about your faith</u>. He can help you work through all the barriers against leading others to him.**

DEPTHFINDER UNDERSTANDING THESE KIDS

You can make faith sharing easier for your kids by guiding them through the process. Use these suggestions from Youth Ministries magazine (Jeff Anderle, "Acceptance + Friendship = Evangelism," Youth Ministries, November/December 1996) to help you support your kids as they develop and share their faith.

● Meet with groups of your students.

● Study the foundational elements of the Christian faith together.

● Take time to pray for specific teenagers.

● Plan outings for outreach to non-Christians.

● Invite non-Christians to fun youth group events.

● Invite non-Christians to Bible studies.

This method might take more time, but its emphasis on developing relationships helps new Christians establish a lifelong commitment to Christ.

DEPTHFINDER

THE SEVERAL HABITS OF HIGHLY EFFECTIVE EVANGELISTS

Here are a few specific approaches to sharing your faith. You may know of some others. Try these—and the other approaches you think of—to "make the most of every opportunity" (Colossians 4:5b). As a Christian, everything you do can be an act of evangelism.

Pray. Whenever you're feeling frustrated or at an impasse, remember that you can always turn to God for help. Although you can open the door for somebody to have a relationship with God, don't forget the role the Holy Spirit plays. Prayer not *only* guides you as you share your faith, but it is sometimes the only thing you can do for someone.

Teach. Be prepared when someone asks you about spirituality or God. As Philip did for the Ethiopian in Acts 8, you can help someone understand God's Word.

Speak. Any time you speak the truth of God's Word, you are sharing your faith. You can debate an issue from a spiritual standpoint. You can talk to your friends about God. Just remember Peter's words of advice: "Do this with gentleness and respect" (1 Peter 3:15b).

Serve. Christ calls us to live out our faith by serving others. When you serve, you're not only taking care of someone's physical needs, but you're also sharing Christ's love with others.

Live. In every action, you may be influencing others. Are you setting an example? Someone may either accept or reject a relationship with Christ based on how *you* live your life as a Christian. That's a huge responsibility, but it's one every Christian faces.

EVANGELISM EXPLORATION ▼

S.H.O.H.E.E. (10 to 15 minutes) Have kids place their chairs in a circle and sit down. Distribute Bibles, and ask a volunteer to read aloud Matthew 28:16-20.

Say: **Jesus is telling us to make disciples, but all of us know how difficult that can be. That's why I'm calling our first meeting of the Several Habits of Highly Effective Evangelists, or S.H.O.H.E.E. Our goal is to learn to effectively share our faith.**

Hand out name tags and pens, and have kids write their names on their name tags and put them on. Say: **Think about what we've just read in Matthew. Let's go around the circle and introduce ourselves by talking about either a reaction to this Scripture or a personal experience—good or bad—that you've had with evangelism.**

Start by sharing one of your own experiences. Then have kids go around the circle, introducing themselves and sharing. Place a large sheet of newsprint and some markers on the floor in the middle of the circle. Ask:

● **Why do you think Christ wants you to tell others about him?**

Have kids take turns writing their answers on the sheet of newsprint. Encourage them to fill the newsprint with as many thoughts as possible.

Challenge students to go beyond obvious answers like "He doesn't want others to go to hell" to deeper answers as found in the "Why We Should Share Our Faith" Depthfinder (p. 38).

Say: **Jesus made clear that we're to share our faith with others, but he also made clear that he'll always be with us. Even though sharing your faith may seem difficult sometimes, God helps you talk about your faith.** Let's learn some effective ways to share our faith. Tape the sheet of newsprint to a wall so kids can refer to it throughout the meeting.

Opportunity Knocks (25 to 30 minutes)

Have kids clear their chairs from the floor. Then scatter on the floor the situation photocopies you made from the "Opportunity Knocks" handout (p. 44) before class. Give a Bible to each person. Say: **Becoming more effective evangelists means we need to be prepared for opportunities to tell others about God.** Explain that each color of paper on the floor has a different situation on it. Explain that when you say "go," two students will go to a sheet of paper, read the situation on it, and then listen for further instructions. Say: **Go!**

After kids have paired up and read their situations, have them read Matthew 25:31-40. As kids are reading, write these questions on newsprint:

● How could you use the approach described in this Scripture to share faith in your situation?
● Would this be an effective approach? Why or why not?
● Can you think of a more effective approach? Explain.

Tape the newsprint to a wall where everyone can see it.

After pairs have read the Scripture, have them discuss the questions on the newsprint. After a few minutes, ask for volunteers to share what they discussed.

Then explain that when you say "go," each student should move to a different color of paper and find a different partner. This time, have pairs look up Ephesians 5:1-2 and discuss the questions on the newsprint you taped to the wall.

Then have kids exchange partners and discuss two more situations using the following Scriptures:

● Colossians 4:2-4
● 1 Peter 3:15-16

Be sure to have pairs share what they discussed after each situation. After the last discussion, ask:

● **What did you learn about how to share your faith with others?**
● **Did you discover any surprising approaches to sharing your faith? Explain.**
● **How can the approach you use help you to share your faith effectively?**
● **Have you ever used one of these approaches before—even if you didn't realize it at the time? Explain.**

Ask for a volunteer to read aloud Colossians 4:5-6. Ask:

● **What does it mean to "make the most of every opportunity"?**
● **How do you feel about using different approaches to "make**

the most of every opportunity" in your own life?

Say: **Some of you may be hesitant to share your faith. Perhaps you just haven't found a comfortable way of doing so.** God can help you figure out a comfortable approach because <u>God helps you talk about your faith</u>. **Now we'll explore another habit of highly effective evangelists.**

CLOSING COMMITMENT ▼

You, Me, and Him (5 to 10 minutes)

Have kids remain in pairs. Say: **Tell your partner about a situation you've faced in which you had an opportunity to tell someone about God. For example, you might tell your partner about a time you heard someone say he or she didn't think God was real.**

After a few minutes, ask:

● **How can your partner encourage you in this situation?**

Distribute paper and pens and say: **One of the habits of highly effective evangelists is that they seek support from others. With your partner, list four ways you can help each other become highly effective evangelists. For example, you could write "praying together," "helping each other recognize opportunities to share your faith," and "studying the Bible together."**

After a few minutes, ask for volunteers to share with the class what they wrote. Ask kids to commit to a time every week to talk to their partners about faith-sharing issues. Encourage them to use and evaluate the four ideas they listed to guide them as they mentor each other.

Then say: **We can help each other learn how to become more effective evangelists, but there's yet another person you need to include in your partnership: the Holy Spirit.** Ask:

● **How do you think the Holy Spirit can help you to be a more effective evangelist?**

● **How can you remind yourself and your partner that the Holy Spirit can help you?**

DEPTH FINDER UNDERSTANDING THE GREAT COMMISSION

Sometimes people miss the significance of Matthew 28:20, when Jesus assures us that he is always with us. Though the focus of the Great Commission is to tell others, Jesus ends this command with words of encouragement. *The Quest Study Bible* explains, "Though physically absent, [Jesus] remains with believers in a spiritual sense. It is his spiritual presence within that strengthens and encourages believers...Those who trust in Jesus will find him with them no matter where they go or what problems they face."

As you encourage your kids to share their faith with others, use Matthew 28:20 to help them understand that God doesn't abandon them; he is with them always.

Say: **As individuals, we look for opportunities to talk about our faith. As Christians, we can support each other in our development as effective evangelists. But ultimately, the Holy Spirit is in charge. No one will make a faith commitment to Christ unless the Holy Spirit is working in his or her life. So don't forget that <u>God can help you talk about your faith</u>.**

Have partners look up Philemon 6 and repeat the verse to each other as a closing prayer.

"Be wise in the way you act toward outsiders; make the most of every opportunity. Let your conversation be always full of grace, seasoned with salt, so that you may know how to answer everyone."

—COLOSSIANS 4:5-6

Opportunity K·N·O·C·K·S

Situation 1

In the lunchroom, you hear a group of kids at the next table talking about evolution. You hear one person say, "Only idiots think a god was in charge of creating this place."

··

Situation 2

A new kid just came to your school. He seems pretty nice, but he's very shy. He's not really an outcast, but it doesn't seem that he has any real friends.

··

Situation 3

You read in the newspaper about a family whose house burned down. The newspaper quoted the father as saying, "We lost everything. Why did this happen to us?"

··

Situation 4

A few weeks ago, your best friend got dumped by his girlfriend. He's still moping around and refuses to hang out with you or his other friends. He keeps saying things like "Nothing matters anymore."

··

Situation 5

Your school's football team just won the championship! Everyone's going to "the hill," and someone says they've raided their parents' liquor cabinet. Your friends are thinking about going.

It's Worth the Price

Helping Kids Share Their Faith in a Hostile World

by Jim  HAWLEY

■ The armed guerrillas stormed the New Tribes mission base in Columbia and kidnapped Steve Welsh and Timothy Van Dyke. A year later, the men were killed during a skirmish between government troops and the guerrillas. The men knew the risks involved in ministering in Columbia, but as Scot Ross, the New Tribes spokesman said, the "risk of lots of people in Columbia dying without having heard about Jesus Christ" was of greater concern to the men. ■ After watching 1,600 people come to Christ during a weeklong rally for reconciliation in Rwanda, Israel Havugimana was murdered by fellow Hutus who opposed his call for tribal reconciliation. ■ Mehdi Dibaj became a Christian as a teenager after reading a tract. The Iranian pastor spent ten years in prison. After his release, he disappeared while heading for his daughter's birthday party. His body was later found in a public park. ■ According to David Barrett, one in every two hundred Christians can expect to be martyred in his or her lifetime ("Modern Martyrs Die for the Faith," Current Thoughts and Trends, December 1995). Persecution is not just a dark time in humanity's past. And it's not just found thousands of miles away. Ask your teenagers what sort of response they get at school when they assert that people who don't believe in Jesus go to hell. Ask them how others respond when they say that Christianity is the only true religion. ■ While your kids don't face the same level of persecution as Christians in China or Iraq, they are sharing their faith in a hostile environment. Your kids face ridicule, disdain, and even violence for reaching out to a hurting world. ■ Use this study to inspire your kids to continue sharing the message of the gospel and to remind them that while sharing their faith isn't always easy, it's vitally important.

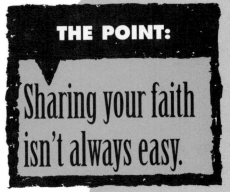

THE POINT:

Sharing your faith isn't always easy.

The Study
AT A GLANCE

the study at a glance

SECTION	MINUTES	WHAT STUDENTS WILL DO	SUPPLIES
Case Study	10 to 15	THE ULTIMATE PRICE—Hear and discuss an account of Polycarp's martyrdom.	Bibles
Simulation Activity	10 to 15	THE LAND OF NO GOD—Experience a futuristic place where believing in God is punishable by death and explore options of living in such a place.	"Nogodland Laws" handouts (p. 53)
	20 to 25	TRUTH ON TRIAL—Defend their faith during a simulated futuristic trial for persecuted Christians.	Bibles, "Trial Evidence" handouts (pp. 54-55), pencils, paper
Personal Encouragement	5 to 10	PERSECUTION PRAYERS—Share examples of persecution and pray for each other.	

notes:

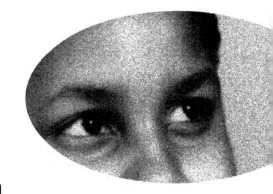

THE POINT OF "IT'S WORTH THE PRICE":

Sharing your faith isn't always easy.

THE BIBLE CONNECTION

EXODUS 20:3-5a	God commands us to avoid worshiping any god but him.
MATTHEW 10:16-28; 28:18-20; PHILEMON 6; and 1 PETER 3:15-16	These passages give instruction on sharing faith.
JOHN 14:6-7a	Jesus states he is the way, the truth, and the life.
ROMANS 1:20-23	Paul reveals how people refuse to recognize God.

In this study, teenagers will study a Christian who died for his faith, experience living in a simulated culture where belief in God is illegal and where their faith is put on trial, and encourage each other with ways to endure persecution today.

Through these activities, kids will be encouraged by examples of faithfulness, gain a better understanding of what they believe, and learn how to handle their faith in a hostile culture.

Explore the verses in The Bible Connection; then examine the information in the Depthfinder boxes throughout the study to gain a deeper understanding of how these Scriptures connect with your young people.

LEADER TIP for The Study

Because this topic can be so powerful and relevant to kids' lives, your group members may be tempted to get caught up in issues and lose sight of the deeper biblical principle found in The Point. Help your kids grasp The Point by guiding them to focus on the biblical investigation and discussing how God's truth connects with reality in their lives.

THE STUDY

CASE STUDY ▼

The Ultimate Price (10 to 15 minutes) Have kids form groups of no more than four. Give kids Bibles and have them read Matthew 10:16-28. Ask:

● **How would feel if you had been one of the apostles Jesus**

LEADER TIP

for The
Ultimate Price

If you have additional time, you may want to explore the martyrdom of the apostles found in the "Fathers of the Faith" Depthfinder (p. 49). Use the questions on page 49 to discuss the apostles' martyrdom experiences.

LEADER TIP

for The
Ultimate Price

Polycarp's martyrdom is a historical fact, but not all of the stories surrounding the event can be proven.

LEADER TIP

for The Study

Whenever groups discuss a list of questions, write the questions on newsprint, and tape the newsprint to the wall so groups can discuss the questions at their own pace.

was warning?

● **What do you think would be the most difficult part of the apostles' assignment? Why?**

● **What is the most difficult thing about sharing your faith?**

Say: **Jesus promised his apostles they would suffer persecution for his name. But many men and women since then have suffered greatly for Jesus also. Listen to the story of Polycarp, a bishop who lived in the city of Smyrna, in the second century.**

Read the following story about Polycarp aloud.

POLYCARP: BISHOP OF SMYRNA

In A.D. 161, Marcus Aurelius became emperor of the Roman Empire. Like previous Caesars, Aurelius persecuted the Christians. His reign ushered in the fourth persecution, to which one of the most famous martyrs, Polycarp, fell victim.

Polycarp was the bishop of Smyrna. Three days before soldiers apprehended him, Polycarp dreamed that the pillow he was sleeping on caught fire and burned up. When he awoke, he told others he would be burned alive for Christ's sake. The church members urged him to flee, which he did, but soldiers found him in a neighboring village a few days later. Surprised by Polycarp's old age and gentle spirit, they granted him an hour to pray. Some of the soldiers regretted that such a godly man would be put to death.

When Polycarp was brought before the tribunal, the proconsul urged Polycarp to save himself in his old age by denying Christ and swearing by the name of Caesar. Polycarp answered, "Eighty and six years have I served him, and he never once wronged me; how then shall I blaspheme my King, Who hath saved me?"

Upon further pressure to renounce Christ, Polycarp boldly affirmed that he was a Christian and told the proconsul he would teach him the Christian doctrine if he would give him a day. The proconsul stated that he would put Polycarp in with wild beasts if he didn't repent. Polycarp answered, "Call for them, for repentance with us is a wicked thing, if it is to be a change from the better to the worse, but a good thing if it is to be a change from evil to good."

Finally, the proconsul threatened Polycarp with fire. Then Polycarp said, "You threaten me with fire, which burns for an hour, and is soon extinguished; but the fire of the future judgment, and of eternal punishment reserved for the ungodly, you are ignorant of. But why do you delay? Do whatever you please."

Then Polycarp was led into the stadium. Crowds of Jews and Gentiles were told Polycarp confessed himself to be a Christian. They furiously shouted, "This is...the father of the Christians, and a subverter of our gods!" When the lion keeper refused to send out any animals, the people gathered wood to burn Polycarp at the stake. When the people tried to fasten him to the stake, Polycarp told them, "Leave me as I am; for he who giveth me strength to sustain the fire, will enable me also, without your securing me with nails, to remain without flinching in the pile." After they bound Polycarp without nailing him to the pole, Polycarp prayed, "O Father, I bless thee that thou hast counted me worthy to receive my portion among the number of martyrs."

After Polycarp's body was burned in the fire, the Christians gathered his bones and buried them in a proper place.

(Taken from *Foxe's Book of Martyrs*)

After the story, ask:

● **What emotions came to mind as you listened to this story?**

● **How do think Polycarp faced martyrdom so nobly?**

● **How do you compare the persecution you may face with that of Polycarp?**

● **What words do you use to define the persecution you face today?**

● **Does the fear of persecution affect how you express your faith to others? Explain.**

● **How can Jesus help you face persecution today?**

Say: **We probably won't have to face the kind of persecution that Polycarp and other Christians faced. But today there are people who are just as closed to hearing the truth of Jesus. <u>Sharing your faith isn't always easy.</u> Let's try an unusual experiment to further explore this idea.**

SIMULATION ACTIVITY ▼

The Land of No God (10 to 15 minutes)

Say: **Welcome to Nogodland. It is the year 2356. Your existence is controlled entirely by powerful society computers run by human servants. From now on, you must follow**

LEADER TIP for Simulation Activity

Consider creating a courtroom atmosphere by using tables, chairs, and additional props. Place a small table with a chair behind it near a wall. Put additional chairs on the opposite side of the table. Make a sign saying "Quadrant 933 Courtroom." Create a futuristic ambiance by placing a TV or computer monitor on the table for the judge to consult and by covering the table with aluminum foil. Make a name tag for each person: "Registered Citizen 356912," for example.

the laws of this land. A friend of yours who serves in the misinformation bureau discovered a Bible on an obsolete computer CD-ROM. After reading the Bible and learning about God and Jesus' resurrection, your friend converted to Christianity.

Your friend has convinced you of the truth of Christianity and is now helping you to share your faith with others. But you've received a memo from the Computer Servants, warning you about your illegal faith and the penalty for sharing that faith. Now you're in a secret meeting with the other Christians, planning ways to share your faith with the registered citizens of Nogodland.

Have kids form groups of up to four. Give each student a "Nogodland Laws" handout (p. 53) and have students read the memo. Have groups discuss the following questions:

- **How would it feel to live in a society that denies God?**
- **As a believer in God, which of the six laws would be hardest for you to follow? Why?**
- **How well could you share your faith with other registered citizens if you obeyed the laws?**
- **What principles would you be willing to die for?**

Give groups five minutes to discuss the questions. Then say: **I wanted to hear your ideas, but I'm afraid I'll hear them at your trial. I've just been informed by the Computer Servants that your illegal activity has been identified and you must answer to the High Ideal.**

—1 PETER 3:15b

"Always be prepared to give an

ANSWER

to everyone who asks you to give the

reason for the hope that you have.

But do this with

gentleness and respect."

DEPTHFINDER

UNDERSTANDING THE BIBLE

In his Gospel, Matthew writes about Jesus' commissioning and sending out the Twelve, to preach to the Jewish people in Palestine. To encourage the apostles who would face rejection, Jesus offered two analogies. The first (Matthew 10:24) involves the relationship between the student and the teacher or a servant and a master. Jesus explained that since he faced persecution as a teacher, the disciples surely would face the same.

The second analogy (Matthew 10:25) offers a striking picture of the intensity of the persecution: If the leader of a household is called Beelzebub, so much more are the household members called Beelzebub. The word "Beelzebub" is recognized in the New Testament as a term for the prince of the demons or Satan. This insult is vile—the Messiah himself rejected as Satan! As this term is used by the Pharisees in Matthew 9:34 as well, the passage suggests this slur against Jesus was frequently used by his enemies. The disciples would be accused of doing Satan's work just as much as Jesus was.

Truth on Trial (20 to 25 minutes)

Form six groups, and give each group one of the defense cards from the "Trial Evidence" handout (pp. 54-55) and a Bible. Have kids keep their "Nogodland Laws" memo. Have each group choose a spokesperson to present the group's defense, an evidence collector to read the group's assigned Scripture, and a recorder to write down the group's defense discussions.

Give groups ten minutes to plan their defense strategies based on their assigned Scriptures and questions. Each numbered defense card correlates to the law with the same number on the "Nogodland Laws" memo. Say: **I am the Computer Servant overseeing this portion of the trial. I will decide the fate of registered citizens charged with violating the laws of Nogodland. Each defendant group will be responsible for defending its decision to violate one of the Nogodland laws. You will present your evidence by answering the questions on your group's defense card.**

Have defendant groups present their evidence. While each group presents its evidence, have the other groups serve as juries, and have them judge the defendants. When all defendant groups have presented their cases, say: **I, the Computer Servant of Quadrant 933, determine you are all sincere in your illegal faith. Because you all violated the laws set forth by the High Ideal, I have authorized the High Ideal Computer to terminate your existence.**

Ask:
- **What was it like to be on trial for your faith?**
- **What did you learn about sharing your faith in this trial?**
- **What sort of persecution would you be willing to face for your faith?**
- **What types of things intimidate or prevent you from sharing your faith right now?**

LEADER TIP
for Truth on Trial

If you have fewer than six kids, have groups take more than one law and defense card as needed.

● **How do you think you would react if this trial were real?**
Say: **You may never have to defend your faith in court, but it**
is helpful to think about where you stand in your commit-
ment to Jesus. Sharing your faith isn't always easy, but
it is tremendously important, and it is worth any type of
persecution we must endure.

LEADER TIP
for Persecution Prayers

If kids explain that they've never encountered persecution for sharing or living their faith, have them talk about times they were afraid or unable to share their faith with someone else.

PERSONAL ENCOURAGEMENT ▼

Persecution Prayers (5 to 10 minutes)
Have kids form pairs. Have one partner share times he or she has faced persecution for sharing or living his or her faith. Then have the other partner pray briefly for him or her. Then have partners switch roles.

After both partners have shared and prayed, say: **You have just**
practiced one of the best ways to help Christians share their faith
with others: prayer. Throughout history, when Christians have
faced persecution for sharing their faith, they have had the
prayers of fellow Christians to encourage them. They
knew, as we do, that sharing our faith isn't always easy.
Prayers are one way we can help one another be bold and
strong.

Close with a prayer thanking God for the help he provides when sharing faith becomes difficult.

DEPTH FINDER UNDERSTANDING THESE KIDS

"**W**hat's true for you may not be true for me."
This statement best sums up the dominant philosophy of today's post-modern culture—relativism. In his book *The New Absolutes*, William D. Watkins illustrates the growing acceptance of relativism using the three most recent research studies by George Barna.

In 1991 Barna found that 28 percent of adults surveyed strongly agreed with the following statement: "There is no such thing as absolute truth; two people could define truth in totally conflicting ways, but both could still be correct."

Another 39 percent somewhat agreed with this statement, bringing the total of people who somewhat agreed or strongly agreed with this statement to 67 percent.

When the study was repeated in 1994, those who strongly agreed with the statement rose to 32 percent, and those who somewhat agreed rose to 40 percent, bringing the total to 72 percent, an increase of five percent in three years.

Those born between 1965 and 1983, labeled the Baby Busters by Barna, rejected absolute truth by 78 percent. Watkins concludes the younger the population, the more inclined it is to accept the philosophy of relativism.

This research shows the hostile environment kids face when sharing their faith. Kids can be encouraged by knowing they need only to *share* their faith by their words and actions, how others *respond* is beyond their control.

NO(GOD)LAND Laws

COMPUTER SERVANTS CORRESPONDENCE

DATE: 2356

TO: All Registered Citizens

FROM: The Computer Servants

RE: Quadrant 933 Annual Law Review

On the ninth day in the fourth month of the year of our High Ideal, 2356, the Computer Servants completed the annual law review for Quadrant 933. All registered persons in this quadrant must adhere to all these laws.

In light of the unfortunate and growing problem of registered citizens adhering to an obsolete religion from centuries past, the laws requiring all registered citizens to have absolute trust in the High Ideal Computer will be strictly enforced. Any and all violations will be recorded by the Society Computers and reported to the Computer Servants. Within three days, all violators will be tried under the supervision of the Computer Servants, overseen by the High Ideal Computer.

ILLEGAL ACTIVITIES FOR REGISTERED CITIZENS:

LAW

1. worshiping and paying homage to anything other than the High Ideal and the inner self

2. sharing any faith unauthorized by the Society Computers

3. discussing of any belief in anything beyond oneself

4. mentioning any obsolete religious terms such as god, jesus, holy spirit, bible, faith, truth, love, heaven, hell, eternity, and creation

5. substituting any other belief for absolute allegiance to the High Ideal Computer

6. encouraging other registered citizens to give up their absolute allegiance to the High Ideal

Any registered citizens found guilty of violating any Quadrant 933 laws will have their existence terminated by the High Ideal Computer.

TrialEvidence

Defense Card 1

Read Exodus 20:3-5a.

Defense Questions:

- How would you paraphrase this passage?
- Why is this passage important to sharing your faith?
- How have you used or could you use the truths in this passage in sharing your faith?
- How have you faced persecution in sharing your faith?
- How will you use your faith-sharing experiences as evidence in your trial?
- How will you use this passage as evidence in your trial?

Defense Card 2

Read Philemon 6.

Defense Questions:

- How would you paraphrase this passage?
- Why is this passage important to sharing your faith?
- How have you used or could you use the truths in this passage in sharing your faith?
- How will you use your faith-sharing experiences as evidence in your trial?
- How will you use this passage as evidence in your trial?

Defense Card 3

Read Romans 1:20-23.

Defense Questions:

- How would you paraphrase this passage?
- Why is this passage important to sharing your faith?
- How have you used or could you use the truths in this passage in sharing your faith?
- How will you use your faith-sharing experiences as evidence in your trial?
- How will you use this passage as evidence in your trial?

Defense Card 4

Read 1 Peter 3:15-16.

Defense Questions:

- How would you paraphrase this passage in your own words?
- Why is this passage important to sharing your faith?
- How have you used or could you use the truths in this passage in sharing your faith?
- How will you use your faith-sharing experiences as evidence in your trial?
- How will you use this passage as evidence in your trial?

Defense Card 5

Read John 14:6-7a.

Defense Questions:

- How would you paraphrase this passage?
- Why is this passage important to sharing your faith?
- How have you used or could you use the truths in this passage in sharing your faith?
- How will you use your faith-sharing experiences as evidence in your trial?
- How will you use this passage as evidence in your trial?

Defense Card 6

Read Matthew 28:18-20.

Defense Questions:

- How would you paraphrase this passage?
- Why is this passage important to sharing your faith?
- How have you used or could you use the truths in this passage in sharing your faith?
- How will you use your faith-sharing experiences as evidence in your trial?
- How will you use this passage as evidence in your trial?

why ▼ Active and Interactive Learning works with teenagers

Let's Start With the Big Picture

Think back to a major life lesson you've learned.
Got it? Now answer these questions:
● Did you learn your lesson from something you read?
● Did you learn it from something you heard?
● Did you learn it from something you experienced?

If you're like 99 percent of your peers, you answered "yes" only to the third question—you learned your life lesson from something you experienced.

This simple test illustrates the most convincing reason for using active and interactive learning with young people: People learn best through experience. Or to put it even more simply, people learn by doing.

Learning by doing is what active learning is all about. No more sitting quietly in chairs and listening to a speaker expound theories about God—that's passive learning. Active learning gets kids out of their chairs and into the experience of life. With active learning, kids get to *do* what they're studying. They *feel* the effects of the principles you teach. They *learn* by experiencing truth firsthand.

Active learning works because it recognizes three basic learning needs and uses them in concert to enable young people to make discoveries on their own and to find practical life applications for the truths they believe.

So what are these three basic learning needs?
1. Teenagers need action.
2. Teenagers need to think.
3. Teenagers need to talk.

Read on to find out exactly how these needs will be met by using the active and interactive learning techniques in Group's Core Belief Bible Study Series in your youth group.

1. Teenagers Need Action

Aircraft pilots know well the difference between passive and active learning. Their passive learning comes through listening to flight instructors and reading flight-instruction books. Their active learning comes through actually flying an airplane or flight simulator. Books and lectures may be helpful, but pilots really learn to fly by manipulating a plane's controls themselves.

We can help young people learn in a similar way. Though we may engage students passively in some reading and listening to teachers, their understanding and application of God's Word will really take off through simulated and real-life experiences.

Forms of active learning include simulation games; role-plays; service projects; experiments; research projects; group pantomimes; mock trials; construction projects; purposeful games; field trips; and, of course, the most powerful form of active learning—real-life experiences.

We can more fully explain active learning by exploring four of its characteristics:

● **Active learning is an adventure.** Passive learning is almost always predictable. Students sit passively while the teacher or speaker follows a planned outline or script.

In active learning, kids may learn lessons the teacher never envisioned. Because the leader trusts students to help create the learning experience, learners may venture into unforeseen discoveries. And often the teacher learns as much as the students.

● **Active learning is fun and captivating.** What are we communicating when we say, "OK, the fun's over—time to talk about God"? What's the hidden message? That joy is separate from God? And that learning is separate from joy?

What a shame.

Active learning is not joyless. One seventh-grader we interviewed clearly remembered her best Sunday school lesson: "Jesus was the light, and we went into a dark room and shut off the lights. We had a candle, and we learned that Jesus is the light and the dark can't shut off the light." That's active learning. Deena enjoyed the lesson. She had fun. And she learned.

Active learning intrigues people. Whether they find a foot-washing experience captivating or maybe a bit uncomfortable, they learn. And they learn on a level deeper than any work sheet or teacher's lecture could ever reach.

● **Active learning involves everyone.** Here the difference between passive and active learning becomes abundantly clear. It's like the difference between watching a football game on television and actually playing in the game.

The "trust walk" provides a good example of involving everyone in active learning. Half of the group members put on blindfolds; the other half serve as guides. The "blind" people trust the guides to lead them through the building or outdoors. The guides prevent the blind people from falling down stairs or tripping over rocks. Everyone needs to participate to learn the inherent lessons of trust, faith, doubt, fear, confidence, and servanthood. Passive spectators of this experience would learn little, but participants learn a great deal.

● **Active learning is focused through debriefing.** Activity simply for activity's sake doesn't usually result in good learning. Debriefing—evaluating an experience by discussing it in pairs or small groups—helps focus the experience and draw out its meaning. Debriefing helps sort and order the information students gather during the experience. It helps learners relate the recently experienced activity to their lives.

The process of debriefing is best started immediately after an experience. We use a three-step process in debriefing: reflection, interpretation, and application.

Reflection—This first step asks the students, "How did you feel?" Active-learning experiences typically evoke an emotional reaction, so it's appropriate to begin debriefing at that level.

Some people ask, "What do feelings have to do with education?" Feelings have everything to do with education. Think back again to that time in your life when you learned a big lesson. In all likelihood, strong feelings accompanied that lesson. Our emotions tend to cement things into our memories.

When you're debriefing, use open-ended questions to probe feelings. Avoid questions that can be answered with a "yes" or "no." Let your learners know that there are no wrong answers to these "feeling" questions. Everyone's feelings are valid.

Interpretation—The next step in the debriefing process asks, "What does this mean to you? How is this experience like or unlike some other aspect of your life?" Now you're asking people to identify a message or principle from the experience.

You want your learners to discover the message for themselves. So instead of telling students your answers, take the time to ask questions that encourage self-discovery. Use Scripture and discussion in pairs or small groups to explore how the actions and effects of the activity might translate to their lives.

Alert! Some of your people may interpret wonderful messages that you never intended. That's not failure! That's the Holy Spirit at work. God allows us to catch different glimpses of his kingdom even when we all look through the same glass.

Application—The final debriefing step asks, "What will you do about it?" This step moves learning into action. Your young people have shared a common experience. They've discovered a principle. Now they must create something new with what they've just experienced and interpreted. They must integrate the message into their lives.

The application stage of debriefing calls for a decision. Ask your students how they'll change, how they'll grow, what they'll do as a result of your time together.

2. Teenagers Need to Think

Today's students have been trained not to think. They aren't dumber than previous generations. We've simply conditioned them not to use their heads.

You see, we've trained our kids to respond with the simplistic answers they think the teacher wants to hear. Fill-in-the-blank student workbooks and teachers who ask dead-end questions such as "What's the capital of Delaware?" have produced kids and adults who have learned not to think.

And it doesn't just happen in junior high or high school. Our children are schooled very early not to think. Teachers attempt to help kids read with nonsensical fill-in-the-blank drills, word scrambles, and missing-letter puzzles.

Helping teenagers think requires a paradigm shift in how we teach. We need to plan for and set aside time for higher-order thinking and be willing to reduce our time spent on lower-order parroting. Group's Core Belief Bible Study Series is designed to help you do just that.

Thinking classrooms look quite different from traditional classrooms. In most church environments, the teacher does most of the talking and hopes that knowledge will transmit from his or her brain to the students'. In thinking settings, the teacher coaches students to ponder, wonder, imagine, and problem-solve.

3. Teenagers Need to Talk

Everyone knows that the person who learns the most in any class is the teacher. Explaining a concept to someone else is usually more helpful to the explainer than to the listener. So why not let the students do more teaching? That's one of the chief benefits of letting kids do the talking. This process is called interactive learning.

What is interactive learning? Interactive learning occurs when students discuss and work cooperatively in pairs or small groups.

Interactive learning encourages learners to work together. It honors the fact that students can learn from one another, not just from the teacher. Students work together in pairs or small groups to accomplish shared goals. They build together, discuss together, and present together. They teach each other and learn from one another. Success as a group is celebrated. Positive interdependence promotes individual and group learning.

Interactive learning not only helps people learn but also helps learners feel better about themselves and get along better with others. It accomplishes these things more effectively than the independent or competitive methods.

Here's a selection of interactive learning techniques that are used in Group's Core Belief Bible Study Series. With any of these models, leaders may assign students to specific partners or small groups. This will maximize cooperation and learning by preventing all the "rowdies" from linking up. And it will allow for new friendships to form outside of established cliques.

Following any period of partner or small-group work, the leader may reconvene the entire class for large-group processing. During this time the teacher may ask for reports or discoveries from individuals or teams. This technique builds in accountability for the teacherless pairs and small groups.

Pair-Share—With this technique each student turns to a partner and responds to a question or problem from the teacher or leader. Every learner responds. There are no passive observers. The teacher may then ask people to share their partners' responses.

Study Partners—Most curricula and most teachers call for Scripture passages to be read to the whole class by one person. One reads; the others doze.

Why not relinquish some teacher control and let partners read and react with each other? They'll all be involved—and will learn more.

Learning Groups—Students work together in small groups to create a model, design artwork, or study a passage or story; then they discuss what they learned through the experience. Each person in the learning group may be assigned a specific role. Here are some examples:

Reader

Recorder (makes notes of key thoughts expressed during the reading or discussion)

Checker (makes sure everyone understands and agrees with answers arrived at by the group)

Encourager (urges silent members to share their thoughts)

When everyone has a specific responsibility, knows what it is, and contributes to a small group, much is accomplished and much is learned.

Summary Partners—One student reads a paragraph, then the partner summarizes the paragraph or interprets its meaning. Partners alternate roles with each paragraph.

The paraphrasing technique also works well in discussions. Anyone who wishes to share a thought must first paraphrase what the previous person said. This sharpens listening skills and demonstrates the power of feedback communication.

Jigsaw—Each person in a small group examines a different concept, Scripture, or part of an issue. Then each teaches the others in the group. Thus, all members teach, and all must learn the others' discoveries. This technique is called a jigsaw because individuals are responsible to their group for different pieces of the puzzle.

JIGSAW EXAMPLE

Here's an example of a jigsaw.

Assign four-person teams. Have teammates each number off from one to four. Have all the Ones go to one corner of the room, all the Twos to another corner, and so on.

Tell team members they're responsible for learning information in their numbered corners and then for teaching their team members when they return to their original teams.

Give the following assignments to various groups:

Ones: Read Psalm 22. Discuss and list the prophecies made about Jesus.

Twos: Read Isaiah 52:13–53:12. Discuss and list the prophecies made about Jesus.

Threes: Read Matthew 27:1-32. Discuss and list the things that happened to Jesus.

Fours: Read Matthew 27:33-66. Discuss and list the things that happened to Jesus.

After the corner groups meet and discuss, instruct all learners to return to their original teams and report what they've learned. Then have each team determine which prophecies about Jesus were fulfilled in the passages from Matthew.

Call on various individuals in each team to report one or two prophecies that were fulfilled.

You Can Do It Too!

All this information may sound revolutionary to you, but it's really not. God has been using active and interactive learning to teach his people for generations. Just look at Abraham and Isaac, Jacob and Esau, Moses and the Israelites, Ruth and Boaz. And then there's Jesus, who used active learning all the time!

Group's Core Belief Bible Study Series makes it easy for you to use active and interactive learning with your group. The active and interactive elements are automatically built in! Just follow the outlines, and watch as your kids grow through experience and positive interaction with others.

FOR DEEPER STUDY

For more information on incorporating active and interactive learning into your work with teenagers, check out these resources:

● *Why Nobody Learns Much of Anything at Church: And How to Fix It,* by Thom and Joani Schultz (Group Publishing) and
● *Do It! Active Learning in Youth Ministry,* by Thom and Joani Schultz (Group Publishing).

your evaluation of

Bible Study Series
for junior high/middle school

the truth about
SHARING FAITH

Group Publishing, Inc.
Attention: Core Belief Talk-Back
P.O. Box 481
Loveland, CO 80539
Fax: (970) 679-4370

Please help us continue to provide innovative and useful resources for ministry. After you've led the studies in this volume, take a moment to fill out this evaluation; then mail or fax it to us at the address above. Thanks!

• • • • • •

1. As a whole, this book has been (circle one)

not very helpful   very helpful
1   2   3   4   5   6   7   8   9   10

2. The best things about this book:

3. How this book could be improved:

4. What I will change because of this book:

5. Would you be interested in field-testing future Core Belief Bible Studies and giving us your feedback? If so, please complete the information below:

Name _____

Street address _____

City _____ State _____ Zip _____

Daytime telephone (____) _____ Date _____

THANKS!